D1509365

REAL-WORLD PROJECTS

TO EXPLORE

WORLD WAR I AND THE ROARING '20s

rosen publishing's

rosen central®

New York

HEATHER MOORE NIVER

Published in 2019 by The Rosen Publishing Group, Inc.
29 East 21st Street, New York, NY 10010

Copyright © 2019 by The Rosen Publishing Group, Inc.

First Edition

Library of Congress Cataloging-in-Publication Data

Names: Niver, Heather Moore, author.
Title: Real-world projects to explore World War I and the Roaring '20s / Heather Moore Niver.
Description: New York : Rosen Central, 2019. | Series: Project-based learning in Social Studies | Includes bibliographical references and index. | Audience: Grades: 5–8.
Identifiers: LCCN 2017056523| ISBN 9781508182252 (library bound) | ISBN 9781508182269 (pbk.)
Subjects: LCSH: World War, 1914–1918—Juvenile literature. | United States—History—1919–1933—Juvenile literature.
Classification: LCC D522.7 .N58 2018 | DDC 940.3—dc23
LC record available at https://lccn.loc.gov/2017056523

Manufactured in the United States of America

CONTENTS

INTRODUCTION

A little over one hundred years ago, one of the world's most terrible wars began. World War I is also known as Great War and the War to End All Wars. It was so bad that people thought there would never again be such a war. More than twenty-five countries got involved before the end. More that eight million soldiers and sailors died in this war, and more than twenty million suffered injuries. Between armies, navies, and air forces, more than sixty-five million soldiers assembled to fight. Civilians pitched in, too, helping to manufacture supplies such as guns and ammunition. Civilians had never participated in the war effort to this extent before. Their work was so essential to the war that World War I was considered a "total war," because just about everyone pitched in to help in some way.

As is now obvious, World War I was hardly the last horrifying war the world would ever see. In fact, its peace treaty, the Treaty of Versailles, helped cause yet another terrible war:

OVER THERE

Artist Albert Sterner captured the patriotic feeling of American men who were sent to fight for their country in World War I in this 1917 poster.

World War II. Between these two horrific wars, though, was a time of newfound freedom and community. Women, who had stepped up to fill vacancies in employment, found that not only were they plenty capable of doing so-called "men's work" outside the home, but they also liked it. They liked the challenges, the paycheck they earned with their own brainpower and sweat, and the freedom of having their own jobs. When men returned home and took back their jobs, many women found other employment opportunities instead of meekly returning to a life in the home.

Some headed out to speakeasies, to let loose at last: to drink prohibited liquor, smoke cigarettes, and dance to sizzling hot jazz music in their short, knee-length dresses. Not all women took to the flapper lifestyle, but the freedoms of the corsetless outfits and short, no-nonsense hair stuck around. Radios buzzed with music, news, and much more as their popularity spread across the country. Soon everyone was listening to jazz, sports, news, and more from their homes. Other new technologies came into the home, too, like electric appliances, changing the way people lived, worked, and played.

One of the best ways to learn about the lives and times of people during the Roaring '20s and World War I is to delve into their depths through project-based learning. Project-based learning is simple. Students gain information and skills by working on an involved project that allows them to immerse themselves in the topic and engage with it fully. Projects are designed around captivating, often multilayered questions designed to encourage inquisitiveness and inspiration.

In this resource, readers will discover varied sample projects to use as models for their own project-based learning projects. Some are creative, whereas others are more analytical, providing a balanced selection. Although concrete, specific projects centered on World War I and the Roaring '20s are provided here, project-based learning stresses and encourages imagining original projects. So if students are inspired by one of these projects to go off in a new direction, that's perfect. Feel free to use these examples as a place to get started, and just see what thought-provoking places your imagination leads you.

CHAPTER ONE

MURDER LEADS TO WAR

In 1914, the countries of Austria-Hungary and Serbia had not been friendly neighbors in quite some time. Some Serbians wanted all Serbians living in Bosnia, which was part of the Austro-Hungarian Empire, to unite and no longer accept Austro-Hungarian control. A Bosnian Serb named Gavrilo Princip shot and killed Archduke Franz Ferdinand and his wife on June 28. Princip was one of a group of nationalists who were desperately trying to put an end to the rule of Austria-Hungary over Bosnia and Herzegovina. Because Franz Ferdinand was the Austro-Hungarian emperor's nephew, and next in line to the throne, the repercussions were severe. Just one month later, Austria-Hungary used his assassination as an excuse to get back at Serbia for wanting to unite into a single Serbian state. It accused Serbia of masterminding this crime and declared war against it.

ASSASSINATION OF AN ARCHDUKE

The archduke of Austria-Este, Franz Ferdinand—or Francis Ferdinand as he is sometimes known in English—was born December 18, 1863, in Graz, Austria. His death on June 28, 1914, would trigger the most horrifying war the world had yet seen. His uncle, Franz Joseph, was emperor of Austria-Hungary, and after his father's death, Franz Ferdinand was next in line for the throne. The archduke was outspoken about his opposition to any kind of unification by any of the empire's numerous ethnic groups. On a visit to Sarajevo with his wife, Sophie, Nedjelko Cabrinovic, a Serbian nationalist, tried to bomb their car. It rolled off and injured others instead. Later that day, Gavrilo Princip had better luck with his assassination attempt when he shot straight into their car.

QUESTION: HOW DID SO MANY COUNTRIES ACROSS EUROPE GET DRAWN INTO THE FIRST WORLD WAR?

After the assassination of Franz Ferdinand, both Austria-Hungary and Serbia immediately asked their allies for help. Austria-Hungary called on Germany and Italy, the other members of the Triple Alliance. While Germany entered the

Per tutti gli articoli e illustrazioni è riservata la proprietà letteraria e artistica, secondo le leggi e i trattati internazionali.

Anno XVI. — Num. 27.　　5 - 12 Luglio 1914.　　Centesimi 10 il numero.

L'assassinio a Serajevo dell'arciduca Francesco Ferdinando erede del trono d'Austria, e di sua moglie.

After the assassination of the Archduke Franz Ferdinand, Austria-Hungary retaliated against alleged perpetrator Serbia and triggered the biggest war the world had ever seen.

war on the side of Austria-Hungary, Italy initially stayed neutral. However, the Ottoman Empire, now known as Turkey, sided with the Central Powers, as the Austria-Hungary and Germany coalition became known.

Serbia, a small country, was protected by Russia, which plead its case to its Triple Entente allies, France and the United Kingdom. This group became known as known as the Allies. Other countries that joined the Allies included Italy, Japan, and eventually the United States (after 1917). The Allies went on to win the war.

Germany attacked Belgium on August 4, 1914. In response, Great Britain, which had sworn to defend Belgium, made good on its promise and declared war on Germany. It wasn't long before most of Europe was involved in one way or another.

PROJECT
MAPPING THE MAJOR PLAYERS

Research which countries, both major and minor, were involved in World War I for any time. Then make a map that tracks the quickly evolving geography of the war.

- *Make a list compiling all of the countries that fought in the war.*
  - *What reason(s) did each have for entering the war?*
  - *What about any that decided to leave the war?*

- *Did any countries change sides at any point during the war?*
- *Were there any that made a pointed effort NOT to join? Which ones and why not?*
- *Write down any other interesting facts about the war you come across in your research.*

- **Find a map of Europe that depicts the countries that existed during World War I.**
- **Compile your information using a free online mapping program like http://www.esri.com/software/mapping-for-everyone.**

- *Map out all the countries involved, indicating which side they were on by color, pattern, or other feature.*
- *Designate those with special circumstances (leaving the war, etc.) with other colors or patterns.*
- *Label your map with the year(s) each country was active in the war.*
- *Annotate your map with interesting facts you discovered during your research. Try to find at least one interesting fact for each country.*
- *Include a key to show what each color or pattern used on the map means.*
- *Present it to the class, showing the map on a screen and going through each country individually, explaining the highlights.*

QUESTION: WHAT EVENTS BROUGHT THE UNITED STATES INTO WORLD WAR I?

Not all major countries were so eager to jump into the First World War. The United States, for example, did not join until 1917. At first, the country decided to remain neutral. Most felt that this war did not concern them—it was between "old world" countries. Also, because the United States is a country of immigrants, there were too many associations with both sides. It could get confusing fast.

In 1915, however, some opinions changed when 159 Americans were killed during a German attack that sunk an ocean liner, the *Lusitania*. In total, 1,198 innocent passengers died. Two years later, this loss was still fresh, and many were recruited to join the war with the line "Remember the *Lusitania*."

Then, in January 1917, a second hit came. A telegram intercepted and decoded by the British revealed that Germany's foreign secretary, Arthur Zimmerman, was suggesting to Mexico's German ambassador that if Mexico were to join them and ally against the United States, they would be gifted with Texas, New Mexico, and Arizona. Known as the Zimmerman Telegram, it inspired US president Woodrow Wilson to ask Congress to declare war on Germany in a speech on April 2 and "fight for the ultimate peace of the world." Four days later, the United States made an announcement: it was at war with Germany. (The United States did not officially join the Allies but referred to itself as an "associated power.")

This newspaper headline reports on Germany's sinking of Britain's ocean liner the *Lusitania*, in 1915. Later, the United States recruited soldiers to fight with the slogan Remember the *Lusitania*.

And they were just in time. The Allies were suffering. Everyone—Allies and Central Powers alike—was exhausted and needed soldiers. Once the United States joined the war, the firepower, resources, and soldiers it contributed made a huge difference for the Allies.

When the United States joined the war, President Wilson made history with his Fourteen Points. The only leader who went public with his goals for the war and plans for peace, he included in the Fourteen Points the establishment of the League of Nations, which would hopefully prevent future wars.

PROJECT
EXTRA! EXTRA!

Imagine you are a top columnist for an American newspaper just as World War I is unfolding. Archduke Franz Ferdinand and his wife were just recently murdered and Serbia has been blamed by Austria-Hungary and other countries. There are two clear sides to this war, and you have the opportunity to write an opinion piece for your paper. Are you in favor of the United States joining in the war (pro) or against it (anti)?

- *Use the internet and resources at your local library to look up some primary sources, such as newspaper or magazine articles that were published in the United States (or other countries) as the war broke out. Ask a librarian how to use microfiche or other resources in the library to find the kinds of articles you are looking for. Try to find three prowar articles and another three antiwar articles.*
- *After you have found and read your six articles, think about which side most influenced your thinking.*
- *Write down between five and ten reasons why you think the United States should or should not enter the war.*
- *Write up a one-page column (of at least 250 words) explaining your opinion.*

The library, as well as the internet, are excellent sources for research using primary sources, such as newspapers and magazines that were published at the time.

- *Lay out your article using newspaper-style columns and fonts, naming your column and the newspaper and adding other creative details.*
- *Print out copies of your article for the class and read it for them.*
- *After you have read the article, explain your opinions and why you disagreed with the other side. Ask the class for their opinions, too.*

CHAPTER TWO

EARTH, SEA, AND SKY

The First World War was like nothing anyone had seen before. In part, this was because of the sheer magnitude of the war. But it was also one of the first wars to be fought on land, at sea, and in the sky. And in each theater, new and more potent weapons and vehicles were used. Battle strategies and tactics were also new and more devastating to the enemies. More people than ever were involved in this war. And more people than ever died or were injured.

The Royal Navy of Great Britain had always dominated the seas. It outnumbered Germany's navy, and its warships were more powerful to boot. This allowed Great Britain to create effective naval blockades—but Germany had an ace up its sleeve. The Imperial German Navy had added U-boat submarines to the mix. This turned out to be a lethal addition. It was a German U-boat that infamously sunk the *Lusitania*. U-boat attacks so seriously hurt the British navy that it got down to only six weeks' worth of supplies because so many ships failed to return home. So the Allies changed tactics. They started mounting guns on their boats as well as sailing in groups, or convoys, that were protected by warships. Still, six thousand Allied ships were lost and thirteen thousand died in just the UK naval forces.

Germany was also succeeding with its air force. Floating aircraft called zeppelins bombed the United Kingdom until the British invented special aircraft guns that could successfully take them down. Germany was the first to drop bombs from airplanes, terrorizing British citizens in cities such as London, where around 1,300 died and another 3,000 were wounded from the bombs.

> ## QUESTION: HOW DID WOMEN ADDRESS ISSUES AND PROBLEMS DURING THE WAR, SUCH AS THE LACK OF MEN TO FILL JOBS WHEN THEY WENT OFF TO FIGHT AND THE NEED FOR ADDITIONAL SUPPLIES AND WEAPONS?

World War I was the largest war that anyone had ever experienced, which meant that more people were involved than ever before. For example, in the United States, so many men went to war that women went into the workforce and did their jobs. Women went to work in offices, in factories, in shops, and on farms, just to name a few. More than a few men were horrified that so many women were working outside the home and even daring to wear pants! But the women worked hard and showed skeptics that they were equal to tasks previously considered to require men! Women grew food and made weapons, which helped supply troops during the war.

Not all women stayed behind to support the troops from home. Some went out and joined the forces as well. Before World

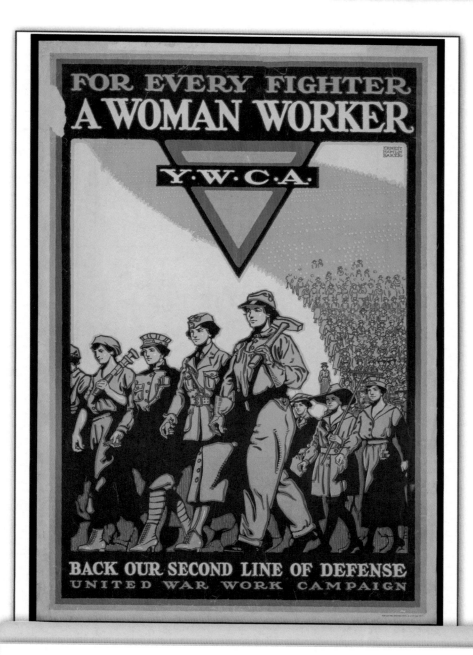

So many men went to fight in the Great War that women filled their positions at home, forming a "second line of defense," as stated in this promotional poster.

War I, the idea of women serving in the military was simply unheard of. The military did not have any accommodations for them. Some women dressed to look like men so that they could go and fight. Others worked as nurses on the front line. None of them received any recognition by the military. But in 1916, the British navy found itself short of manpower. Its fleet had surged from three hundred to one thousand. Happily for women, the language of the Naval Act of 1916 did not prohibit them from joining. The Yeomanettes became an integral part of the navy.

YEOMANETTES

When the British found themselves scrambling for men to populate their rapidly expanding naval fleet, they created the Naval Act of 1916 to expand their options. The language stated that "all persons who may be capable of performing special useful service for coastal defense" could enlist. This phrase left open the opportunity for women to serve. And women did enlist! The navy had to scramble to accommodate the Yeomanettes, or Yeomen (F) as the navy called them, but eventually they were in.

At first women were expected to stick to administrative jobs, and their office skills were tested. But eventually they made their way into work as mechanics, driving trucks, decoding cryptography, operating telephones, and making artillery. But their work did more than just fill personnel vacancies. In the five years that they were active, they showed men what they could do.

PROJECT
VLOGGING TOWARD VICTORY

Women contributed to the war effort in many different ways. Research the stories of individual women during World War I and then try to put yourself the shoes of a couple of these women.

- Research the various ways that women were able to take part in the war effort.
  - In the military
  - At home
- Find some firsthand accounts for each, and make notes. Some questions to consider for each woman might include the following:
  - How did this woman become involved in the war?
  - What country did she live in and what side was it on?
  - What was her life like before the war? Had she ever worked outside the home?
  - How did she make the transition? Was it difficult?
  - What were her duties?
  - What was a day in her life like?
  - What challenges did she face?
  - Did she know other women who were working outside the home?
  - What general issues did she face during wartime?

- *Using your notes, create a diary of a woman working in a war weapons factory, as well as one working outside of the home for the first time.*
- *For each woman, create a vlog or blog she might send to her husband or her family back home about her new and exciting work. Use a free site or application such as YouTube, Blogger, WordPress, or LiveJournal.*

Researching the experiences of one woman during World War I gives you a better idea of what life was like then.

- *Write or perform a month's worth of entries for each woman (make sure to have at least four entries), describing her life, the changes, and her feelings about the war.*
- *Share your blog and/or vlog with the class.*
- *Ask for feedback. Did any of the information about these women's lives surprise them? Why or why not?*

QUESTION: WHAT INFLUENCE DID NEW TECHNOLOGIES HAVE ON THE WAYS WORLD WAR I WAS FOUGHT?

Even though soldiers communicated using carrier pigeons, World War I saw tremendous strides in new war technologies on the battlefield. It eventually came to be referred to as "the first modern war" because so many new technologies, such as machine guns, tanks, aerial combat, and radio communications, were regularly used in military combat. During World War I, these methods were all used on a scale never seen before. Huge guns, called artillery, were so loud that they could be heard across the English Channel. Almost 75 percent of all deaths in this war were a result of these gigantic guns.

World War I was also the first war in which airplanes were used. Planes were used to spy on the opposing side. They were also used to drop bombs from the air. Some airplanes were adapted so that machine guns could be attached to them. Then these airplanes could be used to gun down enemy airplanes.

Germany struck fear in the hearts of its enemies when it brought out zeppelins, airships that would drop bombs anywhere and everywhere. People were so afraid of them that there were regulations to turn the lights off at night and avoid loud noises. Germany took the lives of more than five hundred people through fifty-two zeppelin air raids. Daytime air raids on British cities were carried out by Gothas, a type of German biplane.

One of the best pilots in all of World War I was the Red Baron, as the British called him. Infamous for his red triplane,

Manfred von Richthofen shot down eighty enemy aircraft before his death. He commanded the best pilots Germany had to offer, Fighter Wing I (Jagdgeschwader 1), better known as Richthofen's Flying Circus because they flew whimsically decorated planes and often moved from place to place by rail. He was known for being a very good shooter and did not take too many risks. He was twenty-five years old when his plane was shot down on April 21, 1918.

Manfred von Richthofen was known as the Red Baron for his red plane and his deadly accurate shooting.

Leergewicht 680kg
Nutzlast 235

Another devastating effect came from chemical weapons, such as mustard gas and phosgene. Their effects were so far reaching that the Geneva Protocol was enacted in 1925, which restricted use of chemical and biological instruments in combat. It is still in effect today.

PROJECT
WILD WEAPONRY

World War I saw all kinds of new technologies, which made it one of the biggest and most notorious wars. Create a catalog of some of the most useful, effective, and devastating technologies used in the war.

- Research the kinds of planes, vehicles, tanks, submarines, and other transport used in World War I.
- Research other new technologies used for the first time, including machine guns and chemical weapons, such as chlorine.
- What did each one do? How was it more effective than or an improvement on previous technologies?
- Create a catalog featuring each technology, weapon, or vehicle.
- Write up descriptions of each item, explaining why it is an improvement over past items and why a country should buy it. Make your descriptions engaging so that someone reading your catalog would want to buy the items.
- What are the drawbacks to each item (if any)? Present these as part of your description, too.
- Create a PowerPoint presentation to share each of your items, and present it to the class. Read your descriptions out loud to the class as you go through your presentation.

CHAPTER THREE

SPIES AND SOLDIERS

Millions of individuals played a part in World War I. Soldiers fought, and many gave their lives, for their countries. Spies and secret agents passed along information. Meanwhile, knitters and other crafters created codes in their work or carried secret messages in their knitting bags. Children pitched in whenever they could, too. Many people were enthusiastic and determined to do their part, no matter where they were.

QUESTION: WHAT ROLE DID SPIES PLAY IN WORLD WAR I?

Most espionage work during the war involved eavesdropping, or listening in on conversations. Cryptography was a popular means of sending information on both sides. Coded messages were sent by telegraph and radio. Some women knitted codes into their projects. The knitters used a pattern of bumps and lines in their stitches to create a message. A grandmother in

MATA HARI

Mata Hari may be one of the most famous World War I spies. She was a Dutch woman named Margaretha Zelle who moved to France and presented herself as Mata Hari, an Indian exotic dancer. She met many important, powerful people through her dancing, from whom she may have gotten information to pass on to secret services. She may or may not have been a spy for Germany during World War I, although the French arrested, tried, and executed her as one in 1917.

Mata Hari presented herself as an Indian dancer and may or may not have been a secret German spy.

Belgium created bumps in her knitting every time a train passed and made a hole for the next. Then she passed on her knitted project to a soldier who was working to defeat Germany. Others embedded information in crafts such as embroidery or hooked rugs.

Some people focused on writing secret codes that they hoped the other side would not break and spent time trying to break the enemy's codes. Mabel Elliott worked for the British War Office as a deputy assistant censor. She found a suspicious message and heated the letter and made words appear. She figured out that they were written using "invisible ink"—lemon juice! Other people worked as secret agents and went under cover to get information.

PROJECT
I SPY: ESPIONAGE

Spies were a major part of World War I. Research some of the spies from the war, focusing on two or more from each side. Remember, some spies worked from home. They did not have to be out on the front lines or mingle among leaders to get their work done!

- *Some questions to think about during your research might be:*
  - *What country were they from?*
  - *What did they do before the war and before becoming a spy?*
  - *How did they become a spy? Was there one experience that prompted it?*
  - *Did they have any special talents to make them good spies?*
  - *What tactics or methods did they use to get their information?*

- *Is there any evidence about how they felt about this work? Were they determined? Were they nervous?*
- *How did they hide their messages?*
- *How did they communicate or pass the messages along?*
- *Were they caught? If so, how and why?*
- *What happened to them? Were they executed or did they go on to live a normal life after the war? Or did they continue to work undercover?*
- **Create a character based on a real-life spy, undercover agent, or cryptographer during World War I. Write a synopsis of your autobiography, focusing on important or exciting events about your subject's life.**

QUESTION: WHAT ROLES DID CITIZENS PLAY DURING WORLD WAR I?

Once the United States joined the war, Americans enlisted to join the armed forces and fight. On the battlefield, many soldiers spent days in muddy trenches. Others flew in air missions or sailed on ships. Some stayed home. Women in particular took up the cause for their country without leaving home soil. Some wrote and reported about it for the press, while others worked in factories at home building weapons or helping with other supplies.

Children were a part of the war effort, too. Some children in Great Britain, for example, helped raise money and

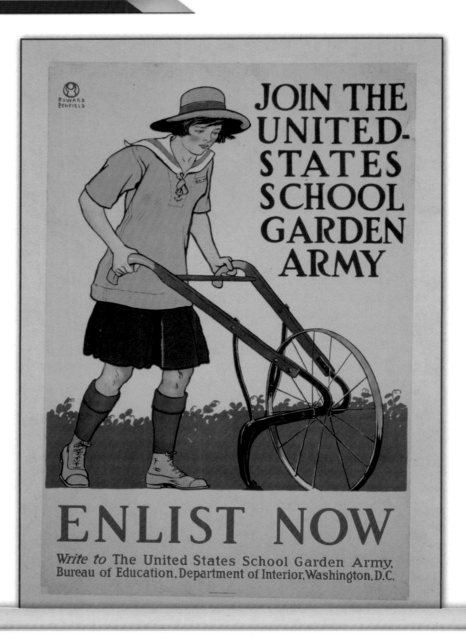

Children found ways to contribute to the war effort, too, such as by joining the United States School Garden Army, which grew fruits and vegetables for leaner times.

donated their own pocket money to the war effort or to charities that cared for wounded soldiers. Others got out their wagons and collected scrap metal. They would go around their neighborhoods and find anything they could. Some even worked on farms or in factories, doing work like building gears. Their work also provided much-needed income for struggling families. Some children grew fruits and vegetables in gardens when supplies were short.

A group of British boys called the Sea Scouts helped by standing watch on the coast when there was a threat of invasion or attacks by Germany. Boy Scouts guarded places that were important to the military, such as telephone and telegraph lines, railway stations, and water reservoirs. Girl Guides sent packages to soldiers, prepared first-aid dressing stations for the injured, and helped out in hospitals, factories, and more.

PROJECT
THEY WERE THERE

The people who lived it tell the best stories of World War I. They may have fought on the front lines, nursed the wounded back to health, or worked at home in factories.

- *Start with your family. Are there any records about anyone in your family who participated in the war? Do your grandparents have any stories passed down from their parents? Consider letters, diaries, or scrapbooks, too.*

Diaries and letters, such as these by Australian lance corporal William Vernon Boase, are an excellent first-person record of the experiences of those who lived through World War I.

- *Another option is to head to the library and research newspaper articles for interviews detailing war work.*
- *Find records, diaries, sketchbooks, autograph books, interviews, or letters from three people who participated in World War I. (Ideally they will have had different jobs, but don't concern yourself too much with this detail because everyone's experience will have been unique.)*

- *Some questions to consider in your research might be as follows:*
  - *What did they do during the war?*
  - *How did they become involved?*
  - *What were their main job duties?*
  - *What was one of the most memorable experiences they had?*
  - *What did they expect? Did things turn out differently than they thought they would? Was there anything that was a total shock or surprise?*
- *Compile your interviews and/or research using free editing programs. Some smartphones have apps you can download or have options to edit within the recording program.*
- *Read your presentation to the class.*
- *Afterward, ask if anyone in the class was surprised by any of the information or experiences of the people you interviewed.*

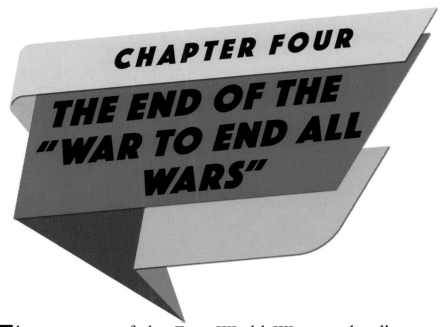

CHAPTER FOUR

THE END OF THE "WAR TO END ALL WARS"

The outcome of the First World War was hardly cut and dry. In the winter of 1917 to 1918, the Western Front was teeming with Germans. But in 1918, the United States was sending around ten thousand troops a day to France. Germany did not take kindly to this shift in numbers and attempted several attacks on French and British troops before the Americans arrived. After an initial triumph at the Second Battle of the Somme, Germany's troops were completely exhausted. The Second Battle of the Marne in July brought an Allied victory that gave them control. By November, they were able to force the German lines back to where they had been in 1914.

Soon various Central Powers surrendered. Bulgaria surrendered on September 29. The Austrians asked for a cease-fire on October 30, and the Ottomans surrendered that day, too. Meanwhile, the Germans were not getting food shipments because of a naval blockade that prevented ships from reaching them. They were desperate and starving. On November 11, 1918, the leaders of Germany's government signed an armistice.

TREATY OF VERSAILLES AND THE LEAGUE OF NATIONS

With the defeat of Germany, US president Woodrow Wilson encouraged the Allies and the rest of Europe to follow his Fourteen Points. He hoped that this would help Europe recover from the war as smoothly and rapidly as possible. However, France and Britain made sure that the Treaty of Versailles was hard on Germany. It required that the Germans pay the Allies a large amount of money and only allowed Germany to have a small army and navy. Later, the Allies also signed individual peace treaties with Austria, Bulgaria, and the Ottoman Empire.

On June 28, 1919, the Treaty of Versailles was signed by German and Allied delegates in Paris. Although the treaty did provide for Wilson's League of Nations, the United States did not sign it because some senators did not approve of the league.

QUESTION: HOW DID GEOGRAPHY INFLUENCE HOW WORLD WAR I UNFOLDED?

The trenches reaching from Belgium to Switzerland, or battlefields to Germany's west, were called the Western Front. Germany was fighting France on this front, which it hoped to do swiftly. But just before the German forces reached Paris, their progress halted. Allied forces pushed them back in September 1914 at the First

Battle of the Marne, which occurred near France's Marne River. Trench warfare went on here for four years!

Two of the war's most horrific battles took place on the Western Front. In 1916, at the First Battle of the Somme, about six hundred thousand soldiers on both sides died, were captured, or were wounded. The frontlines only advanced five miles (eight kilometers) for their efforts. France and Germany also fought a long battle near Verdun.

One of the most devastating fights in the war was the 1916 Battle of Verdun, in Verdun, France. Germany and France fought long and hard for many months.

The Eastern Front was made up of battlefields east of Germany. Here, the action was more fast paced. In August 1914, Russia managed to surprise Germany and moved into its territory. Germany scrambled to move soldiers between Russian troops in Eastern Prussia and drove the Russians out by the end of the month. The Battle of Tannenberg especially hurt Russia. About 250,000 Russians died as the Germans fought back.

PROJECT
MAP MAKER

Make an interactive online map made up of some of the major battles of World War I.
- Choose ten major World War I battles.
- Research these battles, and make notes for each, asking the following questions:
  - Where did they take place?
  - Who were the major players in the war, such as important individuals in the government, military, and so forth?
  - Who won (and lost)?
  - Note any interesting facts about each battle.
- Using a free internet website program or app:
  - Plot each battle on your map.
  - Add captions for each battle, noting dates, the countries involved, and the important facts, individuals, and/or other information you gathered.
- Present your map to the class, moving through the battles in order of occurrence.

QUESTION: HOW DID THE BATTLES, BOTH MAJOR AND MINOR, INFLUENCE WORLD WAR I AS A WHOLE?

Most people expected that World War I would be over after a few short months, but it turned out to be a long, slow war—four years with millions of deaths. Many of those who marched off to war never returned home. A number of those who did make it back suffered from grisly wounds or shell-shock. At home, many of the grieving wives and mothers were forced to shoulder the financial responsibilities for their families.

Some soldiers spent long day after long day after longer day in the trenches. In trench warfare, both sides dig long narrow ditches in which the soldiers hunker down, protected from the gunfire and artillery of the enemy. The closest enemy trenches might only be about 98 feet (30 meters) away! The space between the two trenches was covered in barbed wire and called No Man's Land. Trench life was dismal and dirty. Rats and lice were a fact of life. Latrines overflowed, and sometimes the trenches had many dead bodies in them. Trench warfare caused stalemates for years because neither side gained any ground!

Usually, No Man's Land was very dangerous territory. Sometimes, soldiers were ordered out of the relative safety of the trenches to try and push back the enemy. The scene in some trenches on December 25, 1914, however, was very different. Some German and British soldiers agreed to peace for the day. They got out of the trenches and played games, sang Christmas carols, and chatted for the day!

Fighting from the trenches was not for the faint of heart. It was filthy, exhausting, and treacherous work that might last for years, as neither side gained much ground.

PROJECT
FOUR YEARS AND AROUND THE WORLD

Put together some of the major events with smaller details to compile the big picture.
- *Research major events of World War I.*
- *List twenty major events that you feel had an impact on the war as a whole. For each:*
  - *Write a short summary of the event including interesting details about each event, such*

Researching and compiling minor events together into a timeline helps give a better sense of how World War I played out as a whole.

as what the soldiers experienced in the trenches, on the battlefield, or elsewhere.

* Write a statement about why you feel the event was significant to World War I.
* Select a photo, image, or graphic to use to depict each event.
* Create an interactive timeline using a free online program, such as TimeToast or Timeline JS.
* List each event, with a description and photo.
* Present your timeline to the class, discussing the details of each event.

CHAPTER FIVE

MORE THAN MUSIC AND MAYHEM

The Roaring '20s, as they have come to be known, are famous for their speakeasies; women in short, swanky dresses; hot jazz; and secret consumption and trade of hard liquor. The Eighteenth Amendment prohibited alcohol, which did in fact have some unintended consequences. Americans wanted their alcohol and were apparently not opposed to doing whatever they could to get it. The rise of bootleggers, organized crime, and the speakeasy sets the scene for this time period.

But in truth, the 1920s were a time of far more than just music and mayhem. Women got the vote, marvelous inventions were created, and much, much more. The United States had been on the winning side of World War I, so Americans were relieved, pleased, and confident going into the new decade.

THE "NOBLE EXPERIMENT" OF THE EIGHTEENTH AMENDMENT

In 1919, the US Congress passed a Constitutional amendment that made alcohol illegal effective as of 1920. During World War I, President Woodrow Wilson felt that the grain used to make alcohol would be better used to feed people. So the "noble experiment," as President Herbert Hoover called the period known as Prohibition, made it illegal to manufacture and sell "intoxicating liquors" (but it was not illegal to consume them). The temperance movement latched on to this amendment for its cause to stop people from drinking alcohol. It was not a popular amendment, to put it mildly, and havoc ensued until 1932 when Congress passed the Twenty-First Amendment, which repealed the Eighteenth Amendment.

QUESTION: WHAT NEW INVENTIONS HELPED JUMPSTART THE ECONOMY IN THE 1920S?

The 1920s were a time of economic prosperity in the United States. The economy was thriving! After a positive end to a horrific war, America was now considered a major world power. It was a new beginning in a new decade.

Industry felt the power of positivity, too, and began a period of mass production. Goods like radios, cars, and phonographs were made in great quantities and at lower prices.

In the 1920s, the middle class was able to afford the lower prices of mass-produced items, such as Henry Ford's Model T cars.

The middle class found these items affordable now and bought them. People were even more enthused about new cars with the invention of hard-topped roads. Ford's Model T car cost about $260 in 1925.

New products of convenience were available, too, with the invention of the refrigerator, the toaster, and sliced bread, as well as entertainment like radio and movies. Health improved, too, with the invention of penicillin and the Band-Aid. Business and the economy were booming!

PROJECT
AMERICAN INVENTORS

The exuberance after World War I was expressed in many ways, including in the area of invention. Prosperity meant people could afford more products. Some products were truly ingenious time savers, which allowed people to spend less time on certain tasks and more time (and money) elsewhere!

- *Explore and research inventions that came about in the 1920s.*
- *Choose an invention that you think changed people's lives dramatically during the decade.*
- *Some qualifications to consider might include the following:*
  - *Did this invention improve people's lives?*
  - *Who used it?*
  - *Did it save time?*
  - *Did it save money?*
  - *Did it save energy?*
  - *Did it do a difficult job?*
  - *Why was it special or unique?*
  - *Why or how did it help society or the economy?*
- *Now imagine you are the inventor. Write up a proposal and create a presentation to try and sell your invention to a panel of judges made up of your teacher and four students.*

QUESTION: HOW DID THE ECONOMIC PROSPERITY OF THE 1920S CHANGE PEOPLE'S LIVES AND CONTRIBUTE TO THEIR WELL-BEING?

The 1920s were a time of rapid economic progress, known as a boom. More people owned items like cars, appliances, and homes than ever before. Constant introduction of new products meant new jobs, which fueled this progress. Products could be made faster and less expensively than ever with the use of an assembly line, which was developed by Henry Ford. Electricity was more widely available than ever before, too. Electric products like radios, iceboxes, fans, irons, vacuum cleaners, and lighting created a need for new services. All this production and growth fueled the job market as well as the stock market.

The United States had been in debt to Europe, but everything changed during World War I. America had supplied Europe with ammunition and supplies like food, and now Europe owed them. The United States was prospering.

With better communication and more reliable transportation, Americans were moving in what became known as the great migration. People moved from the country to cities, and many moved from south to north.

Unfortunately, the 1920s did not end on as positive a note as it started. Confident that the stock market would continue to thrive, many Americans made purchases, such as cars, on credit. They thought they would have time to easily pay it back later. People who were active in the stock market kept watching it go up and up and the prices of their stocks were skyrocketing, too.

There's a rhythm in Victor dance music that brings joy with every step

And no wonder! The best dance orchestras make Victor Records—Paul Whiteman and His Orchestra, The Benson Orchestra of Chicago, Club Royal Orchestra, Joseph C. Smith and His Orchestra, The Virginians, All Star Trio and Their Orchestra, Hackel-Bergè Orchestra, International Novelty Orchestra, and other favorite organizations. And such records played as only the Victrola *can* play them make dance music a perpetual delight.

Victrolas in great variety of styles from $25 to $1500.

"HIS MASTER'S VOICE"

Victrola

Important: Look for these trade-marks. Under the lid. On the label.

Victor Talking Machine Company, Camden, New Jersey

Mass production meant that more people could afford luxury items, such as a Victrola phonograph, which sold for as little as $25.

No end to prosperity was in sight! That is, until October 29, 1929. On that fateful Tuesday, now known as Black Tuesday, the stock market crashed, and most people lost their investments. This was the beginning of the Great Depression, a time when many lost their jobs, lost their homes, and went hungry.

PROJECT
SELL IT!

The booming economy in the 1920s can be glimpsed in the many ads that were produced during the decade. Try your hand at crafting a similar ad.

- Research some of the new products that were most popular in the 1920s. Choose one that significantly changed people's lives for the better.
- Imagine you are an advertising executive in the 1920s. Develop a magazine advertisement for a household item that changed the quality of people's lives.
- Some questions to consider include the following:
  - What did it do?
  - How did people handle this task before the item was available?
  - How did this product help people? Did it save time? Money? Energy?
- Create your own original slogan to sell the product.

Researching the types of new products that became available in the 1920s gives you a sense of life during that time.

- *Using a computer graphics program, create an ad or flyer for a magazine to help promote your product. Include images of the product, perhaps showing how it is used or focusing on innovative features.*
- *Present your ad to the class, giving a short three-minute description of the product's best qualities.*

CHAPTER SIX

ALL THAT JAZZ

New products saved money, energy, and time! So with some newfound free time and extra money to spend, people were eager to have some fun, perhaps in an effort to shake off the war's lingering shadows and horrors. During World War I, women had worked hard: they worked outside the home and enjoyed the freedoms that came with it.

But just as women and others were enjoying so many freedoms, Prohibition created limitations. To cope with the prohibition of alcohol sales, people flocked to speakeasies, where they could drink and dance to their heart's content.

QUESTION: HOW DID CHANGES IN COMMUNICATION DURING THE 1920S CHANGE HOW PEOPLE LIVED, WORKED, AND RELAXED?

Jazz and blues music were available across the country, thanks to radio and the availability of phonograph records,

One of the most popular dances during the Age of Jazz was called the Charleston. It was enjoyed by dance enthusiasts young and old.

giving this exciting decade another nickname, the Age of Jazz. People were going out to dance halls to hear—and of course dance to—live jazz bands. This became one of the most popular ways to spend time. New dances like the Charleston, the Shimmy, and the Black Bottom became popular.

The first commercial radio station in the country jazzed up the airwaves in 1920: KDKA in Pittsburgh, Pennsylvania. On November 2, 1920, it broadcast the results of the presidential election, the first live broadcast for the masses. Within three years, the dial was filled with five hundred stations! By the time 1930 rolled around, more than 12 million households spent their time humming along to popular tunes and getting their news on the radio. Radios were so popular that people would stand in line to buy them. Manufacturers could hardly keep up with demand! Soon stations diversified their programming to include much of what we hear today: sports, talks, readings of fiction stories, news, weather, market information, and political commentary.

One of the beauties of radio was that anyone could tune in to it and listen to any kind of program they liked, no matter what the listener's race or ethnicity was. And stations could play anything they wanted, from opera to "race music" (generally the music of nonwhites). So radio resulted in a sense of community. For the first time ever, people on the east coast and those on the west (and everywhere in between) were listening to the same music!

People were also seeing the same movies, thanks to film technology. Film had been popular before the war, but it exploded in the 1920s. By the middle of the decade, US theaters were selling 20 million tickets every week (that's about half the country's population).

Not everyone was so keen on the new technology, new music, and new freedoms of the '20s. As is often the case, some people felt more confortable with traditional types of music and did not care for these new technologies and ways of life. But change was, and is, inevitable.

THE HARLEM RENAISSANCE

Art has been considered an instrument of change, and perhaps this was especially true during the 1920s' Harlem Renaissance. Literature, art, and music all thrived at this time, centered in New York City's Harlem. Previously, the creative work of African Americans had not been given much thought, but now was a time for blacks to be proud of their art. Poets like Langston Hughes wrote about the African American experience. Paul Robeson's booming bass and Josephine Baker's soprano voices rang out, showing audiences throughout the United States and around the world that African Americans had plenty to offer in the arts and beyond. (Both vocalists became activists as well; Baker even worked as a spy during World War II!)

PROJECT
RADIO, RADIO

Radio technology turned out to be a great way to create community.
- *Research styles of music that were popular throughout the decade.*
- *Focus on three distinct styles of music.*
- *Choose songs via a free music website like Spotify and create a playlist of at least nine songs (three from each genre) featuring songs from the 1920s.*

- *Take notes on each type of music. Points to think about include:*
  - *How are the styles the same?*
  - *How are the styles different?*
  - *Who was most likely to listen to each type of music?*
  - *Where was it played?*
  - *Was it performed live, such as in the case of jazz at speakeasies?*
  - *Was it popular overall?*
  - *Did the popularity of radios help spread its popularity?*
- *In class, play one song from each of the three styles you featured. Discuss your thoughts and research on the music.*
- *Make the whole playlist available to the class so they can listen to all the songs you selected after class.*

Radios exposed people to all kinds of popular music. Today we can share music on new technologies.

QUESTION: WHAT FACTORS INFLUENCED THE VIEWPOINTS OF PEOPLE IN THE 1920S?

The work women performed during World War I proved they were up for the jobs. But after the war, men came home and took their jobs back, which put these previously employed women in a tough spot. The benefits offered during the war, such as child care benefits that allowed them to work, were sometimes retracted, so they had to go back to domestic life at home. Many women particularly enjoyed this new independence through working and making money and were unwilling to give it up.

However the decade did bring with it one important new freedom—the right to vote! In 1920, the Nineteenth Amendment was ratified, finally giving women a say in politics. Women were also saying whatever they wanted—using language previously considered "unladylike"—almost wherever they pleased! Many smoked cigarettes (something only men did before this) and drank alcohol. They danced how they wanted. They rode in—and drove—fast cars. Birth control allowed women to take control of their sex lives and gave them the choice to decide if they wanted to wait to start a family.

Women's freedom continued to be expressed through fashion during the 1920s. Women were throwing off their corsets, so they could bend, jump, and dance—move freely! They wore short, slinky dresses they showed their legs up to the knees for the first time in fashion history. They sported short hairstyles, smaller hats, and bold makeup, too.

For most women, the loose-living flapper image was just that: an image. Only a very small percentage of women actually lived

Fashions changed drastically during the Roaring '20s, with freedoms expressed through more confortable clothing and short, practical—yet saucy, as some might argue—hairstyles.

the flapper life. Most women just adopted the fashions, not the racy habits.

PROJECT
THE POSTWAR WOMAN

While the 1920s brought new freedoms for women, the transition to postwar life was not always easy.

- *Research the life of a real woman who lost her job after World War I and learn about her life during the Roaring '20s.*
- *Some questions to consider include:*
  - *What was her work or situation before the war?*
  - *What was her job during the war?*
  - *How long did she do this job?*
  - *Did she like the work? The freedom and independence of having her own job and income?*
  - *What was the work like, and what were the working conditions?*
  - *How did she react or feel about losing her job? Did she expect it?*
  - *What did she do next—how did she cope?*
  - *If she got another job, what was it?*
  - *Was it the same kind of work? If not, describe it.*
  - *Did she have to get additional training?*
  - *If she did not get another job, how did she feel about it? What was her life like after working?*
- *Using a free blogging site, create a blog in the voice of the woman you have researched.*
- *Write at least three blog entries based on your research and own opinions:*
  - *One or more from during the war*
  - *One or more when she loses her job*
  - *One or more to describe her life after losing her job to talk about her new life in the Roaring '20s*

GLOSSARY

armistice A war agreement between two sides to stop fighting for a specific time period.

biplane A type of airplane with two sets of wings stacked one above the other.

blockade A method of preventing food, supplies, or people from moving in or out of a location.

boom A swift rise in economic growth, or widespread success.

cease-fire A brief end to or order to stop fighting, usually to discuss peace.

delegate Someone sent to act as a representative.

diversify To add more variety to something.

espionage The act of spying or making use of spies, such as by governments to gain information from other countries.

flapper A young woman in the 1920s who was considered fashionable while not following traditional rules of behavior.

intercept To get in the way of something in order to inhibit its progress.

manufacture To make a lot of an item, often on machines.

mayhem Forceful or harmful disorder.

nationalist Someone who works for the independence of a country.

neutral Not taking sides or supporting anyone in a conflict.

ratify To formally approve of something, making it legal.

repeal To cancel something out, such as a congressional act.

repercussion An unplanned result, usually after an event has occurred.

stocks An investment of shares of an ownership in a company.

temperance movement A crusade whose goal is to limit alcohol consumption.

theater The place or area where something takes place.

triplane A type of airplane with three sets of wings stacked one above the other.

FOR MORE INFORMATION

Canadian War Museum
1 Vimy Place
Ottawa, ON K1A 0M8
Canada
(819) 776-7000
Website: http://www.warmuseum
.ca/firstworldwar
Facebook: @warmuseum
Twitter: @CanWarMuseum
Visitors can learn about the
more than sixty thousand
Canadians who were killed
in World War I.

Great War Association (GWA)
520 S. Middle Road
Newville, PA 17241
Website: http://www
.greatwarassociation.com
The GWA organization seeks to
keep the memory of World
War I alive and honor those
who served through battle
reenactments and other
educational events.

International Society for First
World War Studies
4 Park Square
Milton Park, Abingdon,

OX14 4RN
United Kingdom
Website: http://www
.firstworldwarstudies.org
Facebook: @FirstWorldWarSoc
Twitter: @FWWsoc
This international organization
of World War I scholars or-
ganizes workshops, confer-
ences, and more to promote
the study of the war that
helped shape the century
that followed.

Library of Congress
101 Independence Avenue SE
Washington, DC 20540
(202) 707-5000
Website: http://lcweb2.loc.gov
/ammem/coolhtml
/coolhome.html
Facebook: @LibraryofCongress
Instagram and Twitter:
@librarycongress
The Library of Congress has
many primary source ma-
terials from the 1920s. The
website listed above records
the Coolidge years, the
nation's changing economy,

and the government's role in it all.

National Organization for
   Women (NOW)
1100 H Street NW, Suite 300
Washington, DC 20005
(202) 628-8669
Facebook and Twitter:
   @nationalNOW
Website: https://now.org/about
   /history/highlights
NOW wasn't founded until
   1966, but it continues to
   strive for equality and rights
   for women and celebrate
   the steps forward made by
   the Nineteenth Amend-
   ment.

National World War I Museum
   and Memorial
2 Memorial Drive
Kansas City, MO 64108
(816) 888-8100
Facebook: @theworldwar
Twitter: @thewwimuseum
Website: https://www
   .theworldwar.org
This museum and memorial

seeks to remember, rein-
terpret, and understand
the war and its effects on
the world through exhib-
its, educational events, the
preservation of historical
materials, and more.

World War One Historical
   Association
2625 Alcatraz Avenue, #237
Berkeley, CA 94705
Website: https://ww1ha.org
Facebook: @World-War-One
   -Historical-Association
This nonprofit organization
   was started in 1911 to help
   spread understanding about
   the war and remember
   those who served and died
   in it.

FOR FURTHER READING

Allen, Frederick Lewis. *Only Yesterday: An Informal History of the 1920s.* New York, NY: Open Road Media, 2015. Ebook.

Bearce, Stephanie. *Top Secret Files: Gangsters and Bootleggers: Secrets, Strange Tales, and Hidden Facts About the Roaring 20s* (Top Secret Files of History). Waco, TX: Prufrock Press, 2016.

Feinstein, Stephen. *The 1920s.* New York, NY: Enslow Publishing, 2016.

Hardyman, Robyn. *What Caused World War I?* New York, NY: Gareth Stevens, 2017.

Lusted, Marcia Amidon, and Jennifer Keller. *The Roaring Twenties: Discover the Era of Prohibition, Flappers, and Jazz* (Inquire and Investigate). New York, NY: Nomad Press, 2014. Ebook.

Mackrell, Judith. *Flappers: Six Women of a Dangerous Generation.* New York, NY: Farrar, Straus and Giroux, 2015.

Morgan, Elizabeth. *World War I and the Rise of Global Conflict.* New York, NY: Lucent Press, 2017.

Rasmussen, R. Kent. *World War I for Kids: A History with 21 Activities* (For Kids). Chicago, IL: Chicago Review Press, 2014.

Samuels, Charlie. *Machines and Weaponry of World War I.* New York, NY: Gareth Stevens, 2013.

Samuels, Charlie. *Timeline of World War I.* New York, NY: Gareth Stevens, 2012.

BIBLIOGRAPHY

CBC News. "World War I Spies Caught by Woman Who Read Invisible Ink." November 10, 2011. http://www.cbc.ca.

The Chicago Radio Show, the University of Virgina. "Radio in the 1920s." Retrieved October 30, 2017. http://xroads.virginia.edu/~ug00/3on1/radioshow/1920radio.htm.

History.com Staff. "World War I History." History.com. 2009. http://www.history.com/topics/world-war-i/world-war-i-history.

Imperial War Museum. "10 Ways Children Took Part in the First World War." Retrieved October 27, 2017. http://www.iwm.org.

National Geographic Kids. "World War I Facts." Retrieved October 2017. https://www.natgeokids.com/uk/discover/history/general-history/first-world-war.

Patch, Nathaniel. "The Story of the Female Yeoman During the First World War." National Archives. 2006. https://www.archives.gov/publications/prologue/2006/fall/yeoman-f.html.

Rosenberg, Jennifer. "Flappers in the Roaring Twenties." ThoughtCo. August 3, 2017. https://www.thoughtco.com/flappers-in-the-roaring-twenties-1779240.

Scholastic. "The United States Turns Inward: the 1920s and 1930s." Retrieved October 27, 2017. http://www.scholastic.com/browse/subarticle.jsp?id=1674.

Trueman, C. N. "Mata-Hari." The History Learning Site. March 6, 2015. http://www.historylearningsite.co.uk.

Wilde, Robert. "Women and Work in World War 1." ThoughtCo. March 27, 2017. https://www.thoughtco.com/women-and-work-world-war-1-1222030.

Zarrelli, Natalie. "The Wartime Spies Who Used Knitting as an Espionage Tool." Atlas Obscura. June 1, 2017. https://www.atlasobscura.com/articles/knitting-spies-wwi-wwii.

Zeitz. Joshua. "The Roaring Twenties." Gilder Lehrman Library. Retrieved October 30, 2017. https://www.gilderlehrman.org.

INDEX

ABOUT THE AUTHOR

Heather Moore Niver writes and edits all types of books for all types of kids. She has written biographies about Sojourner Truth, Ruth Bader Ginsburg, and Ponce de Leon, just to name a few. Niver wrangles words from her log cabin in New York State.

PHOTO CREDITS

Design: Nelson Sá; Layout: Raúl Rodriguez; Editor: Amelie von Zumbusch; Photo Researcher: Nicole DiMella